"What Should I Do?"
Expert Q&A Advice
You Can Count On

By Andrea R. Vander Pluym

SCHOLASTIC INC.

New York Toronto London Auckland Sydney

Mexico City New Delhi Hong Kong

Big thanks to Jim Benning, Sara Fiedelholtz, Erin LeMoine, and Mom. And most especially, thanks to Susan Kaplan and Rita Roth at Anthony Mora Communications.

Cover photo by Jerry Racicot.

ISBN 0-439-06274-8

12 11 10 9 8 7 6   9/9 0 1 2 3 4/0

Printed in the U.S.A.
First Scholastic printing, February 1999

Contents

● ● ● ● ● ● ●

Introduction 1

Chapter 1: Friends 3

Chapter 2: School 23

Chapter 3: Parents 36

Chapter 4: Boys 48

Chapter 5: Siblings 58

Chapter 6: Your Body 70

Chapter 7: Your Emotions 76

Where Else for You to Get Great Information 87

Introduction

This is a very important time in your life. You're beginning to understand yourself, and you're trying to understand others, too. Your relationships with your friends, family, and teachers are changing. Your body is changing as well, or will be soon. The way you feel about boys is also changing.

The questions in this book were asked by girls just like you (they were chosen from a selection of mail sent to *All About You!* magazine by its readers) and, hopefully, you'll find the answers to many of your own questions here, too.

Even if you haven't experienced the same situations discussed in this book, you might have a similar problem. Or maybe you'll have one of these questions in the near future, and wouldn't it be great if you already had the answer?

Chapter 1:
Friends

Q. My best friend is making other friends and spending less time with me. It really hurts. How can I get her to like me again?

A. Just because your friend is making other friends doesn't mean she no longer likes you or that your friendship is less important to her. It's not unusual to have several close friends, especially as you get older. In fact, having many close friends is great because any two people are bound to have some likes and dislikes that are different. Maybe you enjoy ballet and your friend likes soccer, or perhaps you enjoy read-ing books and she likes watching movies. You want to have friends who share your interests, and not one single friend is going to have all the same ones. It's only natural that if your friend joins the soccer team, she's going to make new friends. But it's also true that you're likely to have your own friends from dance class.

What makes your relationship with your best friend special? Do you like to ride bikes together? Do you both like arts and crafts? Think about what makes your relationship with her unique and enjoy what you share with her.

If you still feel like your friend is try-ing to distance herself from you, talk to her about it! If you become quiet around her or stop calling her as much, it might be *you* who causes the relationship to fall apart. Instead, tell her how you feel and that you don't want to lose her friendship. If you do drift apart, it will be hard at first, but at the same time keep in mind that there are a lot of great new friendships to be made!

* * * *

Q. I have a friend who's really nice to my face but then turns around and talks about me behind my back. How can I get her to stop making things up and being so mean?

A. Before you accuse this "friend" of talking behind your back, make sure your information is accurate. Who told you your friend is talking about you? Is it a friend of a friend of a friend? Or is it her best friend who's jealous of you? Or is it your big brother, who likes to tease you?

If the kids who told you are trust-

5

worthy, confront your friend. Calmly tell her what you've heard and that you don't want to believe she would talk behind your back. Ask her what's going on and if it's true. She may deny it. But if you do think she's been gossiping, tell her that real friends don't do that and ask her to explain.

If she does it again, you might want to rethink being friends with her. It won't be easy, and you'll probably miss her despite how poorly she treated you. But if, on the other hand, she admits it and promises to stop gossiping about you, give her another chance if you still want to remain her friend.

It's hard to believe when someone you consider a friend is mean or hurts you. But, at the same time, be sure it's not because of something you did to her first. If you're not to blame, chances are if this friend was gossiping about you, she probably did it to make herself look better. Sometimes people who are insecure try to build themselves up by putting others down. Other times people just aren't nice or they change, and you have to accept that and move on.

❉ ❉ ❉ ❉

Q. My friend tried smoking and now she wants me to try. What should I do?

A. Your friend is probably asking you to smoke with her because she knows deep down that it's not right. When people do something they know is wrong, they often try to involve other people. They figure that if they can get someone else to do it, it's not as bad — or if they get caught, they won't be in it alone.

You shouldn't let your friend pressure you into doing something you don't want to do (this is called peer pressure). Next time your friend asks you if you want to smoke, don't ignore or avoid her by changing the subject or pretending that you have somewhere to go when she pulls out a cigarette. Tell her in a nonjudgmental way that while she might choose to smoke, you know that it's unhealthy and illegal (the law says if you're under eighteen, you're not allowed to smoke) and that you absolutely aren't interested. You may also want to tell her that you wish she wouldn't smoke and that if she's going to, you'd prefer not to be around when she does.

Standing up to peer pressure can be scary — but most kids will respect you when you have the guts to stand up for your beliefs.

* * * * *

Q. I have a friend who's really competitive and likes to show off. It really bugs me. Should I tell her to quit it?

A. If your friend often competes directly with you in a way that hurts you, then you should tell her it bothers you and ask her to stop. When you buy a cute pair of jeans, does she buy two of them just to be "better" than you? When you and your friend get your history reports back, does your friend wave her A+ in front of you? From now on, don't get caught up in her little competitions. Next time she behaves this way, tell her that you're happy when she does well and hope that she's happy for you when you do well. Since you are friends, you don't have to try to top each other all the time. If she wants to compete, tell her she's going to have to do it with someone else.

Q. I always get teased by the popular girls at school. How can I get them to leave me alone?

A. Ignore them — once you've asked them to stop. Hopefully you don't want to be friends with them, because wanting to be a part of their group will make this advice more difficult to follow. You should only have to ask them to stop teasing you once — if you get in the habit of asking them to stop over and over again, they'll just tease you even more. If you haven't asked them to stop already, be sure to ask them in a calm, unemotional way so they don't know how much their teasing really bugs you.

If they continue to tease you, just keep ignoring them. They'll eventually stop, because once you've shown them that it doesn't bother you, they won't find it fun. Usually, the girls who get teased are the ones who react to the teasing. They make good victims.

Do you have your own group of friends? If not, spend time getting to know other kids who could become your friends. When the popular girls see how comfortable you are with your friends, they will be even less likely to pick on you.

However, if the teasing escalates to any kind of physical abuse, such as hitting, or threats of abuse, report it right when it happens to a teacher or other adult you trust. Don't let anyone get away with physically harming you or threatening to.

❋ ❋ ❋ ❋

Q. I have a friend who has everything. I get so jealous sometimes. How can I stop feeling this way?

A. Have you ever heard the saying "The grass is always greener on the other side"? It means that people want what they don't or can't have, and what others have looks so much better to them than what they have. So guess what? Your friend probably does *not* have everything — it just looks that way to you. And it's very possible that there's something you have that she wants. For example, maybe her mom gives her money to buy things, but what she'd really like is for her mom to be home more, like yours is. Or maybe your friend gets to go to summer camp, but what she really wants is to go on a family vacation like you. Everyone has things they want to change about their lives.

Take a look at your life and list all the things you're happy about. Is it family support, great friends, sports or academic awards, or maybe just being able to get out and enjoy the great outdoors? Write all of them down. It's tough to get rid of that jealous feeling altogether, and that's fine. Just keep it under control by looking at your list and realizing that you have a lot more to appreciate than you might have thought.

• • • •

Q. My new group of friends thinks my best friend is a dork. They keep telling me to ditch her, but I really like her — and them. Who should I dump?

A. Hopefully you won't have to dump anyone. After all, your best friend is your best friend for a reason. Think about all of the things you like about her (such as her friendly, caring nature or great sense of humor) and remember them. Then, the next time you're with your other friends and they start trying to convince you to ditch her, you'll be able to tell them with confidence the great things about your best friend. Be prepared to stick up for her and your choice to be her friend.

Have you asked your new group of friends *why* they think your best friend's a dork? Get them to tell you why, and you can then tell them why you think they're wrong. Maybe when your new friends hear about all of your best friend's good points, they'll give her a chance.

It might also be that these friends don't like your best friend because they're jealous that you spend a lot of time with her. So why don't you also tell *them* why you like them just to make sure they're not acting out of jealousy. However, if you stand up for your friend and they still don't like her, tell them it's okay for them to dislike your best friend, but not okay for them to decide your friends for you.

* * * *

Q. Every time I go out for recess with my friends, they break the rules or cheat when we play games. It drives me crazy! How can I get them to play fair?

A. Sometimes people don't like to lose, so they cheat or break the rules. Other times they just plain forget the rules. The best way to deal with these friends is to decide on the rules to your games together beforehand. Your friends will be more likely to play fair when they've helped create the rules. But if they continue to cheat and refuse to play by the rules, you have a choice: Don't take the game seriously or stop playing with them.

Q. It seems like my friends are only nice to me when they want something, like to borrow money or have some of my candy. Are they using me?

A. Being generous is a wonderful and positive quality, but some people take advantage of the generosity of others. If you think this is the case, see what happens when you keep your money at home, or when you don't show up at school with candy. If your friends stop talking to you altogether, then you know for sure that they were just hanging out with you because of what you have, not for who you are. Don't let these "friends" get away with it without calling them on their actions. Tell them that you've noticed that when you don't give them things, that they don't want to spend time with you.

Tell them it really hurts your feelings. If they apologize, you might decide to be friends again. But be careful not to go right back to being super-generous — your friends might be counting on that and be ready to take advantage of you again. Test them for a few weeks by not giving them money, candy, or anything besides the benefit of your company.

• • • •

Q. I have this friend who talks nonstop. She never listens to a word I say. Should I interrupt her and tell her to listen to me?

A. Have you tried being honest with your friend in a nice way? Instead of telling her she's driving you crazy, gently let her know you'd feel more comfortable if you felt like you could talk, too — and that you need a friend who is a good listener as well as an interesting talker. A good friendship is one where both friends feel like they can rely on each other and share their thoughts and feelings — it's not fun when one person takes without giving back.

●　●　●　●　●

Q. My friend always brags about herself. Should I tell her it's annoying and turning her other friends off?

A. People brag for all sorts of reasons, including low self-esteem. But no matter what the reason, there's no getting around how annoying it is when they brag. The best thing to do is to point it out to your friend. Tell her nicely that, while she's your friend, her bragging makes you feel really uncomfortable and unimportant sometimes. You could also let her know that

18

she doesn't need to brag — that you already know how great she is! If her other friends have talked about how annoying her bragging is, be really careful not to bring them into the discussion. Mentioning that they don't like her bragging will only hurt your friend's feelings. She'll think you were all sitting around talking about her behind her back. Ask your friend if she notices when she's bragging, and offer to help her by pointing it out to her when she does it. Remind her again that you're bringing it up because the friendship is important to you — if it wasn't, you wouldn't bother trying to work it out.

* * * *

Q. **My two best friends and I have always been close, but lately they've been getting into a lot of fights. I hate to see them fight, but the worst part is that they always put me in**

the middle. How can I get them both to stop?

A. Don't let your friends put you in the middle of their arguments. It's a very uncomfortable place to be, especially when you like both of them, and you need to let them both know it. Next time they pull you into their argument, interrupt them by telling them you're not going to listen to either of them and that they'll have to deal with it themselves. Tell them you don't want to hear them fight and be mean to each other.

Keep in mind that it's natural that some friendships dissolve. If they end up not being able to like each other, you can still be friendly with them both, just separately. Only be careful not to end up talking negatively about the other person when you're with each friend.

Q. I told my best friend a really personal secret and she went and told it to someone else. I told her off and said things I didn't mean and now she won't speak to me. Who's wrong?

A. It sounds like you both were wrong. You didn't deal with it in the best way, and neither did she — not only did she betray your trust but now she's turning it into resentment toward you and making it seem like it's all your fault. You might be able to fix your friendship by telling your friend how you felt when you found out that she had told someone your secret. Tell her that you had trusted her with something very personal and because you asked her not to tell anyone, it really made you feel betrayed when you found out what she had done. Tell her you really didn't mean the nasty things you said but that you said them because you were so angry at her. Apologize for hurting her and hope that she will forgive you and apologize in turn for betraying your trust.

Chapter 2:
School

Q. The boy sitting next to me in class always copies my tests, but I'm afraid that if I tell on him he'll be mean to me. What should I do?

A. Cheating is a serious thing and he shouldn't do it. However, if you don't want to tell on him, there may be some things you can do on your own to get him to stop. You may not be able to control his behavior but you can change yours. You can try to make sure this boy can't copy your work in a few ways:

• Try sitting in your seat so your back and shoulder shield your tests from his eyes.

- Do you write really big? Try writing a little smaller so it's more difficult for him to read what you're writing.
- When you sense him looking at your work, look him straight in the eye — that might make him feel guilty or at least give the message that you don't like what he's doing.
- Get the teacher to look your way by clearing your throat in an exaggerated way or by squirming around just as the boy starts to look at your work. The teacher might catch on to what's going on and take action without you having to say a word.

If you try these things and you still can't get the boy to stop, then you might want to try talking to him. Say, "I don't like it when you copy off me. Plus, you're not going to learn anything if you're not doing the work." Also, let him know that your answers might not be correct, and that the teacher could find out that he's cheating by noticing his wrong answers are the same as your wrong answers.

If he still continues to copy your work, it's time to tell the teacher. He'll probably get into trouble and might get mad at you. If this boy *does* get angry with you after being punished, say, "I asked you not to copy, but you made the decision to keep doing it. You chose to get caught." You're in a difficult situation, but doing something about it now is the best thing you can do for both you and him. Cheating is the wrong way to get through life, and the sooner he learns this, the better.

• • • •

Q. I don't understand my homework and my parents don't have time to help me. Who else can help?

A. Sometimes parents can seem so busy with their own work or with taking care of younger siblings or with their other chores and responsibilities that you think they don't have time for you. Ask yourself if your parents really *are* too busy, or if you're just afraid to ask them for help because they *seem* so busy. If you don't ask, you'll never know for sure.

There are situations where parents really do have difficulty finding time to help their kids with homework, either because they work long or odd hours or because they have many other family responsibilities that take a lot of their time. And some parents just don't like to help with homework. Or they might feel like the math you're learning is too unfamiliar to them.

If one of these scenarios applies to your situation, try talking to your parents. Say, "I really want to do well at school and I need some help. I'd really like it if you could help me with my homework. If you can't, would you please help me find someone who can?" They might try to help you, or they might try to find an aunt, uncle, grandparent, older student, or tutor who could help you. As far as tutors go, there are lots of options, like on-line tutors and teachers, school-sponsored tutors, nearby tutoring programs, or homework hot lines. See pages 88–89 for two great on-line sources for help with homework.

Homework can be tough sometimes, but try not to give up or get too frustrated. There's help out there, and once you find it you'll be glad you worked so hard for it!

• • • •

Q. I have a difficult time concentrating during class, and I'm always getting into trouble for talking and passing notes. How can I be a better student?

A. Everyone has subjects they like and dislike, so there will often be at least one school subject you're not too interested in. Therefore, during that subject you're probably more likely to talk and pass notes with your friends. You can try to make that boring subject more enjoyable by asking the teacher questions and getting involved. Let's say history is your least favorite subject. Talk to your teacher and let him know you have a difficult time concentrating during class. Ask him how history can be more exciting for you to learn. Perhaps the two of you can come up with special projects that interest you but still focus on the lessons being taught.

There are other possible reasons you're having trouble concentrating: For example, you might have too much on your mind. To beat this lack of concentration, try to clear your mind of other things. If you study, do your homework, and prepare the night before, you won't have to worry as much about a test in another subject that's coming up later in the day or about another homework assignment, and it should be easier to concentrate on the subject at hand.

In addition to coming prepared to class, there are a few other things you can do to help you focus: Make sure you eat right. Don't skip meals. If your body doesn't have fuel to run on, it will be difficult for you to concentrate — especially on subjects you're not too interested in. Also, make sure you get a lot of sleep each night, especially during weeknights. You can't do well if you're not well rested.

If, after trying these suggestions, you're still not finding it any easier to concentrate, ask yourself if there's something else going on in your life making it difficult to concentrate. Perhaps you're distracted by problems at home. Try to remember how long you've had trouble concentrating and when it began. You may want to ask your parents for their advice and help.

● ● ● ●

Q. When the teacher calls on me to do a problem on the board in front of the class, I want to run to the bathroom and hide. Why do I get so nervous and how can I get over it?

A. Getting up in front of a bunch of people can be scary, but guess what? Everyone else is probably just as scared as you when they have to solve a problem on the board or give an oral report. The next time you have to give a report in your science class, for instance, ask yourself what the worst thing is that could happen. Is it forgetting everything you were supposed to say? Or that someone will ask you a question you don't know the answer to? Are you afraid you'll answer a question wrong? Well, any of these can be embarrassing, and having the teacher say you're wrong in front of the class can be humiliating. But it's not the end of the world. You'll feel a little shy or silly, but that's totally normal and these feelings will pass. And keep in mind that it happens to everyone at one point or another. Anxiety about school performance is kind of like going to the dentist: You get all nervous about it and then before you know it, it's over and you're wondering why you got so worried!

If you're prepared, you'll be confident in your abilities. Try to focus on the task at hand and tell yourself that you're going to get up in front of the class, do a great job, and not worry about what the other kids might be thinking. To calm your nerves, take a couple of deep breaths just before you go up and remember that no matter how well prepared you are, it's normal to be nervous. Almost everyone is, including adults. Ask your parents how they feel when they have to make a presentation at work!

* * * *

Q. It seems like I never get chosen when I raise my hand in class or try out for parts in the school play. How can I get my teachers to notice me?

A. Have you tried sitting in the front row? Your teacher will probably be glad to hear you'd like to sit up front so you can be closer to her and participate in class more. Also, take a look at how often you raise your hand. If it's only once a week, you can't expect her to always call on you that one time. But if you're raising your hand several times a day and your teacher still does not call on you, you should talk to her about it. Your teacher may not even realize that she isn't calling on you more often.

When it comes to the school play, make sure you are open-minded about which part you could play. If you're only willing to play the starring role, then that'll lessen your chances of getting a part. Go for any part and you're more likely to be chosen for something.

Another way to get your teacher's attention is by volunteering for things. When she asks for help after an art class, say yes. She'll appreciate your effort and will be more likely to call on you in the future when you raise your hand. Remember, you have to do something — like responding to the teacher or becoming more active — to get noticed!

* * * *

Q. Is there a right way to study and do homework?

A. Because everyone is unique and has different learning strengths and weaknesses, there is no one right way to study or do homework. But here are some tips that might help you to focus and to remember your studies. Try them out to see which ones work for you.

• First off, good study habits begin in the classroom. Listen in class and take lots of notes.
• Try studying a little bit each day to help you remember information bet-

ter. Cramming the night before a test never works as well. Set aside a certain time to review your notes every day, like four to six P.M., and tell your friends not to call you during that time.

• Where you study or do homework is also very important. Make sure you pick a well-lit, quiet, and private place.

• Tackle the most difficult subjects first, while you are fresh and have the most energy. When you're tired, it's harder to concentrate so save the easy ones for last.

Chapter 3:
Parents

Q. **My parents got angry at me when I told them I wanted to quit Girl Scouts. They're always trying to make me do things I don't want to do, and we end up fighting. How can we work things out?**

A. Sometimes it's hard to understand why your parents want you to do something you don't want to do. Believe it or not, your parents usually want what's best for you, even if it doesn't seem that way to you. Have you tried asking them why they'd like you to continue? Maybe there's something else you'd enjoy more that also has some of the positive qualities your parents like about Girl Scouts. You might suggest this new activity to them and see what they say.

As you continue to develop your own interests, you're likely to have other disagreements with your parents. The key is to keep the lines of communication open. If you don't understand why they want you to do something (or why they *don't* want you to do something), you should always ask them to explain. And, in a calm voice, let them know how you feel and why (no whining!). Chances are you will think of a good compromise together — something you all can agree on.

* * * *

Q. My parents are always punishing me. Is that fair?

A. That depends on a number of things. Punishment is fair when your parents have clearly set forth rules beforehand that you've then broken. For example, have they explained to you that if you come home late, you'll be grounded for two days, and if you don't do your math homework, you'll be grounded for a day? If they have, and you come home late or don't do your homework then, yes, it's fair because you've been forewarned.

When is punishment unfair? If you're getting grounded for something that's an accident — say unintentionally letting the dog in the house when it had mud on its paws — then perhaps you'll want to talk to your parents about the severity of their punishment. Another reason grounding might seem unfair is when your parents aren't consistent. Maybe one time they ground you for not doing the Wednesday night dishes, and then they forget to ground you when you break the same rule a month later. This can be very confusing and make it difficult for you to figure out what your parents expect of you.

If you really think a punishment is unfair, talk to your parents. Tell them you'd like to see a list of rules and how you'll be punished if you break them. If you don't agree on the punishment, try to work out a compromise. As much as punishments seem mean or unfair, they can be positive if they can help you to grow and learn from your mistakes.

● ● ● ●

Q. My mom works a lot and makes me do a lot of chores around the house. She says they're my responsibility, but I

don't have time for anything else. Help!

A. Both you and your mom are in a difficult situation. She probably doesn't want to work as much as she does, but because she has to, it puts you in a position where you have to help out with more than you think is your fair share. Do you have any brothers or sisters capable of helping out? If so, are they doing as many chores as you? If not, ask your mother if she could split the chores more evenly and fairly. But if you're the only one available to help, tell your mom how you feel and ask her if it would be possible to change how often the chores are done. For example, if she makes you vacuum twice a week, ask her if you can cut down to once a week. Let her know that you realize she works really hard and needs you to help around the house, but that you don't think it's fair to burden you with so many chores. Let her know that having enough time for schoolwork and friends is also very important to you.

* * * * *

Q. My mom and dad are getting a divorce. It seems like they don't care how I feel. I'm worried about what's going to happen. Should I tell them?

A. When parents are in the midst of a divorce, they usually are distracted and have their minds on a lot of stuff. Sometimes they're short-tempered and unaware that they're hurting the feelings of those around them or perhaps even ignoring the people they love, including you. Even though they're probably preoccupied and upset, it's perfectly fine for you to talk about your feelings and worries with them. Say, "I would like to talk to both of you about how I feel." Your mother and father should then set a time to sit down with you and talk about what's going on. Don't be afraid to tell them how you really feel.

Divorces aren't easy for anyone in the family. Your grandparents and aunts and uncles are probably upset as well. Sometimes children of divorced parents blame themselves for their parents' breakup. If you begin to think things like, "If only I didn't get into so much trouble," or "If only I took better care of the dog," stop yourself and say, "It's not my fault." See, your parents' love for each other — or lack thereof — has nothing to do with how much they care about you.

This is most likely going to be a hard time for you for at least a few months, and probably longer. There might be some major changes in your life. You might have to move or have to choose which parent you want to live with. You might not see one of your parents as much. It's not going to be easy, but there are people who can help you get through your parents' divorce. There are many support groups, including ones where you can talk to other kids your age whose parents are also getting divorced.

Whenever it seems as if your feelings and worries are too much to handle, try to remember that you'll feel a lot better when you talk about your feelings with someone you trust. Have you ever heard the saying "Time heals all wounds"? There's a lot of truth in it. It might take a while, but as time goes by, the divorce will hurt less and less.

● ● ● ●

Q. My mom and dad always want to plan things with me on the weekend, but I don't have as much fun with them as I used to. Now I'd prefer to spend more time at my best friend's house or just be alone to write in my diary or e-mail my friends. I feel bad about it. What's happening?

A. You're growing up! You're discovering who you are, and it's nothing to feel bad about. Your parents know that as you get older, what you like and don't like will change. But even though they may realize you're changing, it's usually not easy for parents to deal with. So try to balance your family time and alone time. Let your parents know that you still love them, but that there are other things you'd like to do as well.

Make a deal with them. Say, "I'll go to the movies with you on Friday night if you'll let me get together with Erin on Saturday night." Remember that your parents have feelings, too, and that while they love who you're becoming, they're going to miss the little girl you're leaving behind.

* * * *

Q. My grandmother just died and I feel horrible. How can I stop crying?

A. Losing someone you love is one of the hardest things you will experience in life. There is no easy way to get over the pain, loss, and loneliness you're feeling right now. But there is a way to take the sting out: Try to remember all the things you loved about your grandmother. Did she tell funny stories or take you to the park? Did she drive you to school (even though you usually walked) on the days it rained? These are good memories, and they'll be with you for the rest of your life. So next time you get sad or begin to cry, remember something about your grandmother that made you laugh or smile or feel loved. Over time, the good memories will begin to replace the sadness you feel. You're very lucky to have gotten to know your grandmother and to have loved her so much — so many people don't have that opportunity.

* * * *

Q. My dad is marrying a really nice lady, but I'm afraid she's going to try to take me away from my mom, who I live with. Can she?

A. If you're happy living with your mother, then you shouldn't worry. And if your father's new wife-to-be is as nice as she seems, then she wouldn't want to take you from a home you're happy living in. It's tough when parents split up and remarry, and it's very common for kids to worry that their home life will change again.

Have you talked to your father about your fears? Next time you're alone with him, tell him how you feel. Tell him that, while you really like your new stepmother-to-be and are glad he's happy, you are also afraid that he and she will want you to leave your mom and go live with them. Make it clear to him that you want to continue living with your mother and he should understand and respect that. And don't be afraid to get close to your new stepmother. You can enjoy mother-daughter activities with her — and even love her — without worrying that you'll lose your real mother or that you'll love your mom any less.

Chapter 4:
Boys

Q. I used to think boys were gross, but now I think I like the boy who sits next to me in class. I feel weird about it. What should I do?

A. When you see this boy, you probably feel like there are butterflies in your stomach, right? Well, don't worry — it's perfectly normal. Many girls your age are beginning to like boys. There are a couple of possible reasons why you're suddenly interested in them. The first is that you may be beginning the transitional period of puberty, when you are physically changing from a girl to a young woman.

Another reason why you might be attracted to this boy is that his behavior toward you has changed. Maybe you didn't like him before because he always acted like a jerk or only wanted to do guy things, like play tackle football in the mud. Is he being nicer now? Do you find him less "gross" because he stopped playing football all the time and started doing something you're interested in, like acting in the school play?

If you want to get to know him better, try being friendly to him. Ask him questions about homework or a report he just gave, or try giving him a compliment. If he doesn't seem interested, don't take it personally. Most boys mature more slowly than girls and go through puberty later, which means he might still think girls are gross. Be patient and try to remember you once felt that way about boys — he will soon catch up.

Q. There's this boy in my class who always teases me. Why does he do this and how can I make him leave me alone?

A. This might seem hard to believe, but this boy is probably teasing you because he likes you. Boys sometimes have a hard time expressing their feelings — they're often too immature to do it in a clear way, so they do it by acting goofy or through teasing. If you're not interested, ignore him. By reacting to his teasing and telling him to stop, chances are he'll just tease you more. After you ignore him a few times, he'll probably get the hint and leave you alone.

But if you *do* like this boy and want to get to know him better despite the teasing, you can try something different. First, engage him in conversation by asking him about something you know he's interested in. Then, once you are talking, it will be easier to tell him that his teasing hurts your feelings. Once he realizes he can have a normal conversation with you, he'll be less likely to tease you. If he really *does* like you, he'll probably want to stop teasing you once he realizes how much it bothers you. If, on the other hand, it turns out he doesn't have a crush on you, then at least you can be happy you stood up for yourself — and maybe you will have gained a friend in the process.

* * * *

Q. **I'm always thinking about boys. Why do I always think about them when I should be doing homework or other things?**

A. First, ask yourself how often do you *really* think about boys. If you think about them a few times a day, that's normal. But if you think about them *every second* of the day — when you're eating breakfast, riding in the car, sitting in class, etc. — there are a few reasons this could be happening. Your body could be going through some big changes and making you feel more attracted to boys. Or it could be you think about boys so much because you're bored. Figure out exactly when it is you think about boys. Is it during your most boring school lesson, like math? If you don't find whatever it is you're doing interesting, it's not surprising that your mind wanders to something that *does* interest you — in this case, boys.

If this is what you think is happening, from now on make a big effort to focus on what you're supposed to be doing whenever your brain starts going into boy mode. If it's a school subject that's boring you, tell your teacher that you're having problems focusing and see if he can help you. Even though it's normal to think about boys, first and foremost, all girls need to love and respect themselves. A great way to tone down your boy obsession is by getting involved in something you enjoy. Are you interested in sports, drama, or an after-school club? Do you spend enough time with your friends? Maybe if you do some things you enjoy that make you feel good about yourself, you won't have boys on the brain all the time.

• • • •

Q. Why does it seem like all boys are mean and disgusting?

A. It might seem like all boys are mean and disgusting because it's the obnoxious ones who stand out. The boy who puts gum in a girl's hair and gets sent to the principal's office is usually more noticeable than the quiet boy in the corner who does all his homework and never gets into trouble. Girls mature faster than boys, so many boys at this age may seem "mean and disgusting" to you when, in fact, they are just a little behind you emotionally. But not all boys are awful — take a look around you and I'm sure you'll notice a few who are fun to be around, but may just be shy. Be friends with those nice boys and ignore the ones who are putting on a show — at least until they grow up a little more! Boys can make great friends, too!

● ● ● ●

Q. My friends like talking about boys, but I don't. Is there something wrong with me?

A. Absolutely not! There are so many other interesting things to talk about. However, if all your friends ever talk about are boys, that can get boring. Next time they start gabbing about boys, try changing the topic by bringing up something you know they are interested in — school, sports, movies, music, etc. If you show interest in the same things they like, you'll probably end up having a great conversation that doesn't revolve around boys. But you have to realize that most girls *like* talking about boys sometimes so you can't expect them to stop discussing them completely. And who knows? Maybe in time you'll want to talk about boys, too. However, if your friends still insist on *only* talking about boys, you probably will want to find other friends who have some of the same interests as you. The friendships that last are the ones where the friends involved have many common interests and like to share them with one another.

* * * *

Q. How can I tell if a boy in school likes me?

A. There are a number of ways. To begin with, the most obvious way to tell if a boy likes you is by his body language — if he looks at you a lot, smiles at you, or leans close to you. Also, does he sit at the same table as you at lunch? Does he manage to stand next to you when you line up? These gestures are often signs that he likes you. Does he tease you?

That could be another signal. Does he get nervous near you? Does he fidget, trip over his feet, or bump into things when he's around you? These are more signs that could mean he likes you. If you think he *does* like you, and you like him, talk to him. Once you let a boy know you're interested in him, he'll usually respond by talking to you more!

Chapter 5:
Siblings

Q. My sister often borrows my clothes and then doesn't return them. Sometimes I find them under her bed and they're ruined! How can I keep her out of my stuff?

A. Your sister needs to learn how to treat your stuff with respect. She might not realize how poorly she's treating your clothes, so gather up some evidence, like a shirt she has stained, then sit down and talk to her. Say, "I would really appreciate it if you'd treat my stuff the way you'd like others to treat your stuff." Show her the shirt and tell her why her lack of respect makes you angry. Ask her how she would feel if you treated her clothes that way. Set some rules for borrowing each other's stuff and discuss how you'll handle it if something gets stained or lost. If a couple of weeks go by and that doesn't work, ask your parents to talk to your sister.

Once you've won that battle, be sure to set your own good example. There might be a couple of things *you* can change about your own behavior to guarantee your sister's respect:

• Ask yourself where your clothes were when she took them. If you toss them on the floor, misplace them, or just don't take good care of them, you're not setting a good example of how you'd like your stuff treated.
• Make sure you're treating her clothes with the same respect you expect from her.

• Keep the lines of communication open. If you think it's possible your sister's been taking your stuff because she's angry about something you did, talk to her. Tell her there are better ways to work out anger.

• Apologize for whatever it is you did (if, in fact, you did insult her) — and ask her to please tell you right away next time she's angry about something instead of taking it out on your clothes!

❋ ❋ ❋ ❋

Q. My brother gets way more attention from my parents than I do, and he gets to do things that I don't. I feel like they don't love me as much as they love him. Why do they love him more?

A. Many brothers and sisters feel the same way you do at times, but it's important to note that getting to do certain things does not define love. First, do your parents even know you'd like to do some of the things your brother is doing? Remember, parents can't read minds, and sometimes they might not be sure what you like to do. Maybe your brother gets to go in-line skating at the beach while you take tennis lessons. If you'd rather be skating like your brother, tell your parents (and try not to whine while asking). If they don't want you in-line skating, don't be afraid to ask why.

Also it might only *seem* like your brother gets to do more stuff. Ask your brother if *he* ever wants to do some of the things *you* do. His answer might surprise you. It's very likely that he's jealous of you sometimes, too, and might even think you get special treatment from your parents at times.

Once you're involved in activities you really want to do, see if it seems like you're getting enough attention. It could have been that the attention you were getting before didn't feel like enough because it revolved around activities you weren't enjoying. However, if you still feel as if your parents really aren't spending enough time with you, tell them — but don't bring your brother into it. Say, "I feel like we don't spend enough time together. I'd like to have you just to myself more often." Chances are, they hadn't realized how you felt and will be grateful to you for letting them know.

• • • • •

Q. My older sister likes to pick fights with me. My mom says I need to ignore her, but

how can I when she makes me so angry?

A. Dealing with anger can be very difficult. There are some great tricks you can learn to help you keep the anger — and your sister — at bay. Identify what it is she says that makes you so angry. Are there topics or words you know will start a fight, like calling you mean nicknames or teasing you about that gross boy she says likes you? If so, you can say to yourself, "Okay, I know that when she says this I get really angry and all it does is get me into trouble." The best thing to do is convince your sister that nothing she says will get you angry. When she sees that she's not getting a reaction out of you, she'll probably stop. But if she keeps teasing you, take a deep breath and walk away. This is difficult to do but it really pays off in the end.

If your sister continues to torment you, here are two ways you can deal with it: Confront your sister and ask her why she picks fights with you. Tell her you would rather get along and have fun together. Or, talk to your parents about it and tell them how hard you've been trying to deal with your sister and your anger. Ask them if you can all sit down together and talk about it.

As much as your sister bugs you, you're really lucky to have one. Eventually, if you can work things out, she might even become your best friend!

●　●　●　●

Q. I have to share a room with my little sister and she's a slob. How can I get her to keep her side of the room clean?

A. Being messy is probably one of your sister's traits — just as being clean is one of yours. You definitely can't *make* your sister change her ways, you can only ask her to. But when you ask her to try to be neater, make sure your requests are reasonable. It's probably not worth making a big deal about it if her only offenses are an unmade bed and shoes that don't line up. However, if she's a total slob who leaves clothes lying around and candy bar wrappers on the floor, then it's worth discussing.

Maybe you can come up with a compromise. You might find that asking her to make her bed every morning is a little too much to ask, but asking her to keep her clothes off the floor is reasonable. Hopefully, she'll try to be a little neater and you'll learn to live with your sister. Try to be understanding and forgiving of your sister's sloppiness. And ask her to understand that you'd like her to try to be a little neater for you. She might just need a little encouragement. Another possibility is to try cleaning the room together — when you have a sister, you can always make a boring task fun by doing it together and joking around! Another option is to help your sister with some of her chores (for example, you could make the bed for her) in exchange for having her help you with something that she likes to do more than you do.

❂ ❂ ❂ ❂

Q. My older brother and his friends are always teasing me. How can I get them to leave me alone?

A. Boys tend to get silly when they're together and they'll sometimes tease someone who's not in their group — especially girls. The best way to get them to leave you alone is to go into another room and do something that doesn't interest them. Or, when you know they're getting together at your house, you could invite your friends over so you're not left alone and a sitting target.

If your parents went out and left it up to your brother to watch you, it's possible he might be a little resentful about having to take care of you. This anger can often come out as teasing — and he and his friends might do it because they want to be alone. If this is the case, tell your parents you'd rather stay at your friend's house when they go somewhere. Try not to feel hurt that your brother and his friends don't want to hang out with you. It's only natural — and you probably do it to your brother when you're with your friends!

Q. My mom just remarried and now my stepfather's son is also living with us! I can't stand my stepbrother. How can I keep him out of my life?

A. Instead of focusing on how to keep your new brother out of your life, why don't you try making him a part of it? Does it feel like you're living with a couple of strangers? By getting to know your stepbrother — and letting him get to know you — hopefully you'll begin to understand each other better. Hey, maybe he feels the same way you do. It could be just as difficult for him. You have to live together, so it's best to try to get along. Plus, you might find that he's a really great person and would make a good friend.

But ask yourself this: Is it possible that you don't like your new stepbrother because you're angry at your mother for getting married again? You probably had no choice in her decision to remarry, and it's possible that it is making you feel unimportant. The next time you and your mom are alone, tell her how you feel. Perhaps you're worried that your new brother won't respect your privacy. Or that your mother won't spend as much time with you as before. When you tell your mom your concerns, be careful not to hurt her feelings. Tell her you're glad she's happy but that you need some reassurance and extra time with her.

Remember, you don't have to love your new family right away (that takes time), but, since you have to live together, why not make the best of it?

Chapter 6:
Your Body

Q. My parents won't let me pierce my ears or wear makeup. Is there anything I can do to look prettier?

A. The best thing you can do to look healthy and beautiful is to make sure you take good care of yourself every day and are well groomed overall. Taking good care of yourself will make you look and feel great.

There are other ways to feel prettier, too.

• Give yourself a new look by getting your hair cut or styled differently.
• Make your hair healthier by using conditioner.

• Keep your hair looking great with regular trims.

• Wear pretty hair clips and jewelry, such as necklaces and rings, to help you feel more attractive. Maybe a splash of fragrance, too.

• Consider wearing clip-on or magnetic earrings as an alternative to pierced ears.

• And don't forget a great smile! A positive attitude does wonders for one's appearance!

* * * *

Q. My mom says I need to start wearing a bra, but it feels like I have a bathing suit on under my clothes. Why do I need to wear one?

A. Girls usually begin to develop breasts between the ages of ten and twelve, though some start developing a little later, in their early teens. There are a few reasons why, regardless of your age when your breasts begin to develop, you should wear a bra.

When your breasts are developing, they can become tender. Wearing a bra helps keep your breasts in place when you're walking, running, or playing sports. Another good reason to wear a bra is because, as your breasts get larger, they can show through your shirts. And once you find a style of bra you like, you'll actually feel more comfortable wearing one.

It's always a good idea to talk about questions you have about your body with someone you trust: your mom, older sister, aunt, or grandmother. You're beginning to experience a lot of changes with your body now, and it will take some time to get used to each change.

Q. I don't like to look at myself in the mirror. I think I'm fat and ugly. What should I do?

A. At this time in your life, when your body is going through a lot of changes, it may be hard to accept some of them. You're also probably focusing more on your appearance because boys are beginning to notice you and other girls. If someone you know is telling you you're fat, don't listen. Everyone's made differently — some girls are tall, some short, some stocky, some skinny. Your body shape and height will continue to change by leaps and bounds as you get older. Try not to be so hard on yourself about your appearance! You'll always find something you dislike about the way you look. Chances are you are much more critical of yourself than others are. The important thing is to be healthy. As long as your doctor says your weight is fine and you are exercising and eating properly, don't worry so much. Instead of focusing on the one thing that bugs you about your body, focus on something you love about yourself. Do you have really pretty eyes or great hair? How about strong arms or nice teeth? Next time you catch yourself putting yourself down, think of these positive traits.

You also might want to do the things that made you happy before you started focusing on the way your body looks. Did you play soccer or read lots of books? Do activities you enjoy. It will make you feel great about yourself and will increase your self-confidence. And it's true that the better you feel about yourself, the better you'll look.

Q. I'm starting to sweat and sometimes smell. What's going on?

A. When you play or exercise, or when it's hot out, your body sweats to stay cool. Underarm odor comes from sweat mixing with the bacteria on your skin. Bacteria usually accumulate in dark, damp places, like armpits and feet. Be sure to shower or bathe after a sweaty day. Some kids don't realize they have to wash more frequently as they get older so it's a good idea to get in the habit of showering daily. Also, to reduce how much you sweat, you can use an antiperspirant. Or, if you don't sweat a lot but are just concerned with odor, you might try a deodorant, which kills germs *and* blocks odor.

Chapter 7:
Your Emotions

Q. My feelings get hurt really easily. Why am I so sensitive?

A. People who are especially sensitive often personalize things too much. In order to toughen up a bit, you need to realize that you can't always please everyone all the time, nor should you try. You really need to work on boosting your self-image and loving yourself. Unfortunately, there will be times when people will say things to purposely hurt you. While you want to make sure you're not being overly touchy, you'll also need to be careful not to blame yourself for everything. It will take some practice, but after a while you'll learn when you're being too sensitive and when your feelings are justified. When in doubt, ask someone you really trust for their take on the situation.

* * * *

Q. Sometimes I feel sad. Is this normal?

A. It's totally normal to feel sad sometimes. Some things that can trigger sadness are friendship problems, frustration with homework, family issues, or even a rainy day!

If you've received a low grade, or if your grandmother is sick, or if you have other problems that are causing you to feel sad, talk to your friends or parents about it. They may be able to help you feel better.

* * * *

Q. I get jealous of my friends a lot. Why do I get so jealous?

A. Lots of times, jealousy has to do with your desire to have what other people have, whether it be good looks, nice clothes, or a special talent. It's okay to admire and wish you also had something that someone else has. But jealousy is harmful when you want that person to lose what it is of theirs that you envy. There's a big difference between admiring something that someone else has versus desiring it for yourself and wanting to take it away from her — that becomes unhealthy and hurtful.

When you find yourself thinking jealous thoughts, take a good look at the situation. Ask yourself what it is you want and why. Do you want that white sweater your friend is wearing because you think it would look cute on you, too, or do you really want to take it away from her because it makes her look too pretty? If your jealousy is causing you to feel anger toward your friends, then you need to examine your feelings. Try to focus on the qualities that make you attractive, like your great sense of humor or your pretty eyes. Appreciate what you have. Your friends might have some qualities that make them beautiful, but so do you! The more you work on examining your own feelings and how you express them, the less jealous you'll become. It will take some time, but if you keep at it, you'll notice a difference and you'll feel more confident and happy.

❉ ❉ ❉ ❉

Q. I'm having a hard time with anger. Sometimes I even throw temper tantrums. How can I learn to control my anger?

A. When it comes to anger, you first have to figure out if it's the actual event of the moment that's making you angry or if you've kept something else bottled up from another time. For example, say a friend tells another one of your friends a secret but she doesn't tell it to you, and this makes you angry. You might pretend like it doesn't bother you but then when you go home and find your sister wearing your necklace you get so angry at her, you end up throwing a temper tantrum. In reality, it's probably the event that happened with your friends earlier in the day — and not your sister wearing your necklace — that caused your anger. See, when you bottle up your anger it usually ends up exploding over something else.

Most people can control their anger if they find the source and deal with it. When you feel like you're about to blow up, take a deep breath and count to three. This can clear your head and help you think about the situation. Ask yourself if it's worth getting upset over. Try to figure out what's really bugging you. Also, think about the person you might be hurting by losing your temper. If you realize you're about to get angry over a minor thing, let it pass and don't give it another thought — not even five minutes later.

Now, you have to deal with those temper tantrums. Do you think that by throwing tantrums you're going to get your way or draw lots of attention to the situation? Well, you might, but only in a negative way. Plus, you're getting too old for tantrums. By now you should be using other, more mature ways to deal with your feelings. When you deal with situations by calmly expressing your frustration instead of acting out, you'll always get a better result.

❋ ❋ ❋ ❋

Q. I'm really shy and nervous when I'm around people. Will that change?

A. Some people are naturally more outgoing and social, while others tend to be shy. There's nothing wrong with being shy but if the shyness bothers you, you can work on becoming more outgoing. The simplest way to lose some of your shyness is to put yourself in situations where you usually become shy. For example, do you get scared when you're called on to read in class? The more you expose yourself to these situations, the more routine and easy they'll become. Let your teacher know that even though you're shy and get nervous, you want to be called on to read more often (perhaps by starting in a smaller group). If you are self-conscious in social situations, like parties, concentrate on asking people questions about themselves to start a conversation. If you're really shy, you'll probably never be one of those types who's the life of the party, but by confronting your fears you should be able to open up, at least a little bit.

* * * *

Q. I saw a scary movie and now I keep having nightmares and I'm afraid to fall asleep. How can I stop being so afraid?

A. Everyone has different levels of sensitivity to what they see. Unfortunately, you can't control your dreams, but you can try to control how you feel when you're awake. There are a few ways to get over your fears. The first is to understand that the movie is just that: a movie. When people go to see a scary movie, it's to be scared. Once you realize it's all made up, maybe the fear will disappear.

If you really have a difficult time getting over it, don't go to scary movies anymore. Did you go this time just because your friends pressured you into going? If so, next time, just say no.

* * * *

Q. **I just moved to a new city, and I don't know anyone! I'm feeling so lonely. What should I do?**

A. It's hard to pick up and move to a new place, leaving your friends and all that is familiar behind. It's even harder when you don't know anyone in your new city. It may seem doubtful right now, but you will eventually settle in, get used to your new home, and make new friends — it just may take some time.

The best place to meet people is in school. So, as long as you are friendly to other kids you shouldn't have difficulty making friends. And once you've met one or two people you can hang out with, you can ask them to introduce you to their other friends. Before you know it, you'll have a whole new group of buds!

However, if the school year hasn't begun yet, then you're going to have to try a little harder to make friends. It's easiest when you focus on your interests and hobbies. Is there a particular sport you're into? If so, you can check out the local recreation center to see if the town sponsors any leagues. If you like biking or in-line skating, ride or blade around areas where other kids go. When you share the same interests, it's easier to strike up a conversation with someone and you're more likely to become friends.

You could also look around your neighborhood and see if there are any kids your age. If there are, introduce yourself. You never know — you just might hit it off and find a new friend!

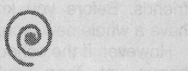

Where Else for You to Get Great Information

• • • • • • • •

Girls Incorporated
National Headquarters
30 East 33rd Street
Seventh Floor
New York, NY 10016
E-mail: email@girlsinc.org
Web site: http://www.girlsinc.org
This nonprofit organization is dedicated to helping every girl become "strong, smart, and bold."

GirlTech
Web site: http://www.girltech.com
This Web site provides links to cool Internet sites that encourage and empower girls to explore the world around them. It has games, features on women in history, "girl views," and much more.

Girl Site
Web site: http://www.girlsite.org
Learn about the world while expressing your own ideas, interests, and concerns.

Girl Power!
Web site: http://www.health.org/gpower/index.htm
Girl Power! is a national public education campaign. It has a superinformative Web site, including great stuff about sports, activities, books, and news — all about girls!

Star Tribune Homework
Web site: http://www.startribune.com/stonline/html/special/homework
Minneapolis–St. Paul's newspaper the *Star Tribune* has a part of its Web site devoted to helping with homework. Its goal is to answer your questions within twenty-four hours, so don't wait until the last minute to ask for homework help! The site covers a variety of different subject areas, including a section on elementary-school topics.

Homework Helper

Web site: http://members.aol.com/Jiskha/ Homework_Help

Have no fear, Homework Helper is here. This Web site has an electronic message board where you can post your questions about homework assignments for any subject! The answer to your question might already be posted, but if it isn't, you'll get a reply in three days to a week.

Kids Health

Web site: http://kidshealth.org/kid/index. html

Got a question that isn't in this book? This Web site has answers for questions about your body, your feelings, and all the changes going on in your life.

For informational pamphlets, contact:
National Health Information Center
P.O. Box 1133
Washington, D.C. 20013
1-800-336-4797

Experts Who Helped with This Book

Joseph Acquaviva, M.D., the vice chairman of psychiatry at Hackensack University Medical Center in New Jersey, is board-certified in child and adolescent psychiatry.

John Bercovici, L.C.S.W., a mental health professional at Hackensack University Medical Center in New Jersey.

Sharyn Hillyer, M.F.T., a relationship therapist based in Los Angeles.

Kathleen Mojas, a clinical psychologist based in Beverly Hills, California; and Matthew J. Pitera, M.D., of Hackensack University Medical Center in New Jersey.

Peter E. Schwimer, L.C.S.W., the supervisor for children's services at the Institute for Behavioral Health Services at Hackensack University Medical Center in New Jersey.

About the Author

* * * * * * *

Andrea R. Vander Pluym lives in San Francisco and is a contributing editor of *Teen* and *All About You!* magazines. Andrea's friends often come to her for advice, and she's always happy to give it!